12 REASONS *to be* GLAD YOU'RE CATHOLIC

I knew something was wrong as soon as I saw the yellow tape. The walkway from the back parking lot to the front of the church was blocked off, and John, the head of our buildings committee, was waving people around the other side.

As soon as I detoured to the front, I saw why. Sometime early in the morning a granite stone about the size of a suitcase had come loose from the upper portion of our church tower, tumbled as it fell, and punched a hole through our handicap access ramp at the side door. There it sat, like a meteorite in a crater, with dozens of gawkers casting their eyes from it, up the tower, and back down. A masonry company was already on the scene stretching a net above the main church door, in case any other stones decided to follow.

Twenty-Third Publications, A Division of Bayard, One Montauk Avenue, Suite 200, New London, CT 06320, (860) 437-3012 or (800) 321-0411, www.23rdpublications.com

ISBN 978-1-58595-894-8

Copyright ©2012 Daniel Connors. No part of this publication may be reproduced in any manner without prior written permission of the publisher. Write to the Permissions Editor. Printed in the U.S.A.

As I stood out front wondering if that little net would even slow down a stone that size, John came around to the front and stood beside me shaking his head. "This tower should have been repointed 30 years ago. Now it's ready to come down in a breeze!"

Six months and a frightening amount of money later, the tower is secure. But you can bet that the forces of wind and rain and snow and ice are already at work slowly loosening and undermining the mortar, and only regular maintenance will save it from falling apart again.

In a way, the same can be said of all of us, the "living stones" (1 Peter 2:5) that are all mortared together into the Church. Instead of water and ice wearing us away, the Church has the collective sins of its billion members slowly wearing away at the spiritual mortar holding us together. Without regular upkeep, our connection to our faith can start to weaken just like that church tower.

How grateful we can all be that Jesus is our cornerstone, the foundation that will never weaken. Staying connected to him through the sacraments is, of course, the primary way to keep our spiritual house strong. But there are other ways too. Sometimes it's helpful to stop and remember all the great things there are about being Catholic. It's easy to complain about what's wrong with the Church, but it would help us all to spend an equal amount of time remembering what's good about the Church, what gifts it's given us, and why, when all is said and done, we're glad to be Catholics.

There are lots of ways to make such a list, and I encourage you to make your own with your family or friends. Here, to get you started, are twelve such reasons, presented in no particular order.

1 COMMUNITY

Many years ago I arrived at Easter Sunday Mass after a long trip to say goodbye to a beloved uncle who was dying. I was tired, and anything but joyful.

When Mass began I stood with hymnal in hand, but the rousing cry of "Jesus Christ is Ris'n Today" died in my throat. I stood there silent, and suddenly became aware of all the voices singing around me. Weak and strong, beautiful or off-key, it didn't matter. I suddenly realized that all these voices were holding me up, singing joyfully to the Lord when I could not sing myself. Their voices helped lift my spirits.

That is one of the great things about our faith community: we are all in this together. Individually, our faith is not always strong. But that's OK. In those times the community as a whole believes for us. We hold each other up. We lovingly pray with and for one another. We draw strength from one another. And at Mass we ask Jesus to "look not on our sins but on the faith of your Church."

It is the community born of Christ's sacrificial love that upholds us. In fact, we would never even have heard of Jesus without the community that has told his story and passed the opportunity for faith from generation to generation. Its saints inspire us, and we've inherited the wisdom it has gained from 2000 years of striving to be faithful to our Lord. It is as part of the community that we gather to worship, and it is through the community that we are all caught up and transformed by the Holy Spirit into the body of Christ.

There are many different roles and ministries in this community, and they're all something to be grateful for. Some of us serve the community as ordained clergy, presiding in our sacramental worship, exercising servant leadership for the good of the community, encouraging and supporting all the faithful as they take up their own paths of discipleship, and connecting us all to one another in the worldwide body of Christ.

Some others of us serve the community as religious brothers and sisters, teaching and caring, praying, spreading the faith, and serving the poor. Some serve as lay ministers in parish life, others in our vocation as in the evening, Matt puts his arms around Ann and says simply but tenderly "You are my wife." Ann returns the embrace, saying "You are my husband." Their children roll their eyes, glad their silly parents have finally figured this out, but for this couple it's a profound and holy moment that takes them back into the heart of their relationship. No matter what they're going through, it reminds them of who they are together and what it means to be husband and wife.

I have long thought that, in that simple ritual, Matt and Ann have captured some things that lie at the very heart of Catholic spirituality. We have many ways of praying and many rituals—in fact, we have many ways of defining and expressing what "spirituality" even means. We speak of Benedictine spirituality, Franciscan spirituality, priestly spirituality, lay spirituality, and many others. But no matter the "brand" of Catholic spirituality, Matt and Ann's small ritual points to at least three central gifts that they all have in common.

The first gift of Catholic spirituality is that, no matter the particular nuance, *relationship* is the hub that holds it all together. Any form of Catholic spirituality may help me explore the deepest recesses of my soul, but it is never really just about me or just about who I am. It's also about you, and who you are, who God is, and who we all are together. Catholic spirituality builds holy relationships. For married couples like Ann and Matt, Catholic spirituality is rooted in being husband and wife and in learning through their marriage to give of oneself out of love for the other. Whether we learn this in marriage or in another state in life, the message is the same: we are not the center of the universe. Catholic spirituality is always relational. It's about being connected, in relationship with one another and with God, who is three persons in one divine relational community.

Sorry about the language there. Writers often find themselves falling back on phrases like "holy relationships" and "divine community" because our Catholic faith is so profound that we end up having to use all sorts of symbolic theological language to try to describe it.

But symbolic language can hide how real and down-to-earth all Catholic spirituality is meant to be. It doesn't foster relationships in theory, but in real life—with all the joy and pain and messiness that real life brings. That is true because of the second great gift of Catholic spirituality—the real, historical event known as the "paschal mystery": the birth, life, death, and resurrection of Jesus that brings redemption to the world. The paschal mystery is Jesus giving himself out of love—even to dying on a cross—so that others might have life.

We enter into the paschal mystery through the sacraments, but all of Catholic spirituality is rooted in it: it means joining ourselves to Christ so completely that we learn to love as he loves, so that we can "die" to ourselves and rise to new life in him. It means learning in love to empty ourselves of privilege and self-centeredness and respond to the world with a growing sense of loving compassion and healing generosity. It means practicing patience and forgiveness. It means taking real life and real relationships seriously and learning to be who we are and are becoming: Christ, in all varied situations and events of our lives. Ann and Matt may not be thinking of this as they carry out their evening ritual, but it is at the heart of marital and every other kind of Catholic spirituality.

It's not always easy to live this way. While Christ has redeemed the world, that redemption isn't yet fully visible. The world is so full of sin and brokenness that well-meaning people sometimes want to draw a very sharp line between what is holy and what is not, what is of heaven and what is of earth. This kind of thinking can lead to an other-worldly spirituality where little good is seen in the things of this world.

While sometimes tempted by it, the Church has always pulled back from that approach. Instead, it has passed on to us the third great gift of Catholic spirituality, what modern writers have dubbed the "sacramental worldview": the prayerful awareness that, while sin and brokenness are indeed real, everything—and everyone—around us contains the potential for holiness, and that everyday, down-to-earth things like water, oil, bread, and wine can help bring us a profound experience of God.

In the sacramental worldview, water isn't always just water: in the font of baptism, we see it as the watery grave in which we die with Christ and rise to new life in him. It is the warm womb from which we are born into the body of Christ. It is living water, flowing, splashing, and gurgling with the very life of God. Oil isn't always just oil. In the sacraments, it is the means by which the Holy Spirit is poured onto and into us. And by the power of that Holy Spirit, bread and wine aren't always just bread and wine. In the Eucharistic liturgy they become the very Body and Blood of Christ himself.

In similar ways, the people we encounter, the work we do, the world around us, the embrace of our spouse or friend—all in different ways offer us the possibility of divine encounter and an opportunity to grow in holiness.

Relationship, paschal mystery, sacramental worldview—from roots such as these grow a wide variety of Catholic spiritualities, spiritualities that have nurtured saints and changed the world.

4 SACRAMENTS

We were stuck in traffic at mile 315 of a 400-mile trip. We had passed mile 314 about an hour ago, and mile 316 was only a vague hope.

My wife, Deb, tried to comfort little Michael, awake and crying in his car seat. We were traveling back to my hometown to have him baptized, and right now we weren't feeling the joy.

For a hectic month we'd been getting ready for this: going through the classes in our current parish, making sure the proper Church records were being transferred back and forth between our Virginia parish and my hometown Connecticut parish, engaging in long-distance planning with family, friends, and godparents. Now, stuck, frustrated, and tired, we just wanted it to be over.

The next day, the baptism itself went much more smoothly. We left the church with our new little Christian and headed off to the party, happy and glad to have it all behind us.

But it wasn't behind us at all. Something else, something mysterious, happened to Deb and me during that baptism. It took us by surprise.

We talked about it later. We knew in faith that baptism would change Michael. We just never expected it to change us as well. But, in some mysterious way, it did. We already loved our son and would have given our lives for him, but when we stood at the font with him in the presence of the community—when we made our promises to unfold the mysteries of faith for him and help him grow as a member of the Church—we felt something changing in us. We left the church with a sense of mission and purpose we hadn't felt before. We weren't just parents anymore. We were *Catholic* parents.

How surprising God can be! While we were occupied with all the planning and driving, we never expected that faint yet powerful touch of God.

Each sacramental moment is indeed the powerful touch of God. It can't easily be seen, and often we don't even feel it, but every such moment undertaken in faith brings us face to face with Christ and plunges us more deeply into the paschal mystery. Baptism is the start. In baptism we become part of Christ and empowered to live his life, to join our own dyings and risings to his, to begin to die to ourselves so as to live more fully for others. The same is true in all our sacraments: confirmation, matrimony, holy orders, and the repeatable sacraments of Eucharist, reconciliation, and anointing of the sick. Each sacrament has its own meaning. Each in its own way offers us the opportunity for transformation. But each—if we open ourselves to the power of the Spirit—

shapes the divine life of the paschal mystery within us, so that more and more, over the course of our days, we can join St. Paul in saying, "I live, no longer I, but Christ lives in me" (Galatians 2:20).

What I've said here is just a very small part of what these sacraments mean. No one understands all of it—all of the richness and depth of these free gifts of God. It's important to learn more about each of them. But the only way to even *begin* to understand them is to receive them in faith and do our best to live them every moment, every day. We may not see any difference in us, but it's there, and someday we may look back and be astonished by where these powerful touches of God have taken us.

5 | EUCHARIST

I have trouble concentrating at Mass. I always have. I'll be listening to the gospel and all of a sudden my mind will jump to why my computer is taking so long to boot up these days or what the traffic will be like when I drive to my parents' home later that day.

This is normal, I know, and when I become aware of it, I gently bring my focus back to the Mass, at least until the next distraction comes along. Sometimes I'm lucky, and in those moments of focus a phrase from the Scripture or from a prayer will hit me right between the eyes.

That happened one Holy Thursday. My mind wandered off during the gospel of the washing of the feet, and I brought it back just in time to hear Jesus ask: "Do you realize what I have done for you?" I suddenly realized I could spend the rest of my life struggling to answer that question.

"Do you realize what I have done for you?" As the gathered assembly shows, Jesus has broken down every barrier to whom we should consider our neighbor, our family. Their joys and sorrows are ours.

"Do you realize...?" In Jesus' paschal mystery—his life, death, resurrection—sins are forgiven, redemption is won, and cries for freedom are answered.

"Do you realize...?" Jesus has taken off his robes and humbly washed our feet, cleansing and redeeming sinful humanity. And he invites us to do the same, to live his redeeming life, to approach one another humbly, to put whatever gifts we have at the service of one another, and to find life in his name.

"Do you realize...?" Christ invites us all, no matter how broken or lame, how rich or poor, friends or strangers. He invites us to be a community of forgiven sinners, to be united in him, to be nourished by his own Body

and Blood, and to be strength and nourishment for one another.

"Do you realize…?" In every Eucharistic liturgy, Jesus gives us an opportunity to recommit to our baptismal promises, to say Yes! to being part of the People of God. He gives us an opportunity to recommit to proclaiming his redeeming death in every aspect of our lives.

"Do you realize…?" When we come to Mass, when we recommit ourselves to being disciples of Jesus, all our lives are changed, even if we don't see it or feel it. Through the transforming power of the Spirit we are absorbed into the body of Christ, all making our prayer of praise to God the Father through, with, and in Christ, and sharing the meal, which is Christ himself. And we are not alone. Our Mass is part of the great Eucharistic liturgy shared all over the earth, and with all the saints in heaven. The whole body of Christ is with us, joined in Christ our head, offering praise to God and interceding for the life of the world.

None of us can grasp the full meaning or implications of the Eucharist, even if we don't lose our focus. But there is supreme importance in realizing that God calls us together at Mass to do in ritual what we are called to do every day of our lives: to immerse ourselves in Christ's death and resurrection, to remember always what God has done for us, to reconcile, to feed and to be fed, to work for justice, and to praise and proclaim by word and deed that God's love is stronger than sin and death itself.

"Do you realize…?" Every Eucharist—indeed, every moment of life—gives us new opportunities to ponder that crucial question, and to be thankful that Christ in the Eucharist, by the very gift of himself, gives us the strength and nourishment we need to keep answering it anew.

6 | PRAYER

A couple of years ago I worked with an author who was writing a simple book about prayer. The book was called *The Catholic Way to Pray: An Essential Guide for Adults.* The book took 120 pages just to offer a very brief outline and summary of our major forms of prayer, from liturgical prayer to litanies to the Scriptural meditations known as *lectio divina*.

Do you like to pray? Then be glad you're Catholic, for our prayer tradition is rich, varied, and insightful. There are prayers of praise, of lament, of intercession, of sorrow and repentance, of adoration, and many more. No matter what you are facing, we have a prayer style for you.

There is, first, liturgical prayer, the official prayer of the community found in the sacraments and the Liturgy of the Hours. This type of prayer is the primary way we enter into and participate in the paschal mystery.

There is devotional prayer, not official for the community as a whole, but essential nonetheless, focusing on Mary, the saints, Stations of the Cross, the crucifix, eucharistic adoration, the rosary, and more, each having the ultimate goal of bringing us the consolations and comforts and challenges of faith, so that we may always be drawing closer to Christ and forming our lives in his image.

Since Vatican II many Catholics have taken enthusiastically to Scriptural prayer. Many of them meet in small groups to share their faith as they reflect together on the readings of the Mass. Others ponder them on their own. And one of the goals of the new translation of the Roman Missal is to help us all realize more fully how deeply the prayers of the Mass are steeped in Scripture.

The spiritual traditions of the various religious orders feed into our great treasure of Catholic prayer, and more and more Catholics are realizing how their whole lives—in their homes, neighborhood, and work—are meant to be offered up as prayers of praise to God.

We can all be glad for Catholic prayer. Rooted in the spirituality we looked at earlier, such prayer can help us realize what is so easy to forget—that we live our whole lives in the presence of our loving God.

7 JUSTICE/CHRISTIAN WITNESS

Herb Woods was a very old man when I knew him. If you watched him totter around town leaning on his cane, you would never guess that he could be counted among the greats in the American labor movement. He wasn't a firebrand on picket lines. He was a lawyer who, working behind the scenes in the '20s and '30s and as an under-secretary in the Roosevelt administration, protected workers in court and helped shape laws that protect us still.

When I was chatting with him one day, the subject of religion came up. "You know," Woods said, "I worked with a lot of religious leaders, and a lot of them didn't understand what the workers were talking about. They had their heads in the clouds. But the priests I knew, they were really sharp. They stood by their people. They had a sense of this world as well as of the next."

Those priests who stood by their people as they worked for justice in the workplace also had the Church standing by them. From the late 19th century until today our popes have led the Church in developing a strong body of social teaching.

From the rights of workers to the care of immigrants, from looking out for the poor and sick to working for legislation that helps and not harms the most vulnerable among us, from racial equality to a strong stance for life at all its stages, our Church strives to live the words it proclaimed at Vatican II—that the Church shares "the joy and hope, the grief and anguish of the people of our time, especially of those who are poor and afflicted in any way" (Constitution on the Church in the Modern World).

The Church's justice/Christian witness is not something tacked on to Catholicism. It is solidly rooted in both Scripture and Tradition, in the God-given dignity inherent in every human being, and the awareness in faith that what affects any one of us affects Christ—and all of us as well, for we humans are all connected to one another.

The social teaching of the Church, of course, can often cause conflict for Catholics. Even when we agree on principles, faithful Catholics of good will often disagree on the best ways to put those principles into practice. But all of us can take justifiable pride in our Church's social teachings. They are the gospel in action. They're a great reason to be glad we're Catholic.

8 | SCRIPTURE AND TRADITION

When I was young and first living on my own, a young couple tried to get me to convert to their church by pointing out how poor I was. They told me that how much money I made said a lot about how strong my faith was, and they proved the point with Scripture—a quote from the third letter of John: "Beloved, I wish above all things that you may prosper." So, they told me, "God gives prosperity to those who love him. So if you're not wealthy or don't drive an expensive car, we know you really don't believe. You need to turn to Jesus!" Really?

Every time I think of that encounter, I remember how glad I am that we as a Church take a different approach to interpreting Scripture, and that we also rely on a 2000-year Tradition to help us interpret it. Both these essential, lifegiving sources, Scripture and Tradition, come from Christ through the power of the Holy Spirit.

Both sources together help us stay away from fundamentalist approaches to faith. They help us respond to cultural needs without falling into the traps of cultural fads (even though our historical track record is a bit uneven here). They guide us as we strive to stay faithful to our Lord in our own time.

We can also be proud of a long tradition of bringing the best of human reason into dialogue with Revelation. Despite some bumps in the road, philosophy and theology have thrived in Catholicism, and Catholics can take pride not only in the Church's intellectual depth but also in the role it has played in the rise of science—from 10th-century Pope Sylvester II, one of the greatest mathematicians of his day, to today's Catholic scientists working at the Vatican Observatory and in labs all around the world. Again, with a few inevitable bumps in the road, faith and science coexist quite well in Catholicism.

Probably all of us can point to some Church teaching that we're not entirely comfortable with, or some issue on which we wish Church teaching would evolve more quickly. The Holy Spirit doesn't work on our timetable and we're *all* capable of resisting what the Spirit tries to teach us.

But I think we can all be glad that our Church takes Scripture and Tradition so seriously and weighs them so carefully. At the very least it can help keep us from some of the crazier stuff—like judging faith by the price of our cars.

9 | CREEDS AND CATECHETICAL RENEWAL

At the Easter Vigil in Constantinople in the year 379, Bishop Gregory Nazianzus was just beginning to speak to the assembly about Christ's resurrection, when a mob broke into the church, swinging clubs and swords and throwing rocks. The Christians inside the church pulled out their own weapons, and soon the building was littered with the bodies of the dead and wounded from both sides.

Was this a pagan mob attacking Christians? No, it was a Christian mob, Christians who disagreed with those inside the church about the divinity of Christ.

Such violence was often common, on all sides. Hints of early splits and disagreements among Christians can even be seen in the writings of the New Testament. From the time of St. Paul, we Christians have been a quarrelsome bunch, hardly ever showing the unity Jesus prayed for. We've fought over just about everything, and even today we've got battle lines set up on lots of fronts. We may not be killing one another these days, but we still have our nasty moments.

But think how much worse it would be today if the Church had not struggled so hard to establish the creeds we so often take for granted today. The creeds are a tremendous gift to us from our faith community. They don't explain the mysteries of faith—nothing can do that—but they guide our reflection on them and establish the boundaries about what is within the truth of our faith and what is not. They are the treasured possession of the whole Church. They help us stay together. And when we proclaim them at Mass, they are a glorious prayer of praise, recounting all the wonderful things our loving God has done for us.

The Church has reflected on the marvelous deeds of God for almost two thousand years, and sharing in those same reflections can enrich us in so many ways. Today, with the *Catechism of the Catholic Church* and all the great catechetical resources and parish programs available to us, we have more opportunities than ever before to learn about the faith we share, to struggle with understanding its truths so that we may help move it forward for future generations, and to let its wisdom, joy, and challenge guide our lives.

10. ECUMENISM

When my wife was in Catholic elementary school, each Monday morning the teachers would ask each child if they had been to confession and to Sunday Mass. My wife always got one additional question: "Did you convert your mother?"

My wife's dad was Catholic, her mom Protestant. They were married in a rectory because such a mixed marriage couldn't be celebrated in the church building.

They supported each other in their different faith practices through their long and happy marriage, but their daughter was often reminded in school that she would miss her mother in heaven, because Protestants just didn't go there.

It's still possible to find Catholics who believe Protestants go to hell because they are Protestants, and one large group of Lutheran congregations in the U.S. still has an official doctrine declaring the pope to be the anti-Christ. But thanks to work undertaken by various Protestant and Eastern Orthodox groups, and—on the Catholic side—to Popes Leo XIII, Pius XI and XII, and the work of the Second Vatican Council and the popes since then, the Church has become increasingly sensitive to Jesus' prayer that all his followers may be one.

Ecumenical marriages always face special challenges, especially when the spouses take their own faith traditions very seriously. The same is true of Christian denominations as a whole. That's why various groups of theologians and leaders of various faith communities continue to sit down together and undertake the very hard and difficult work of dialogue and searching for common ground. Sometimes common understandings are reached, even if the churches remain far apart on other beliefs and practices.

In the meantime, the pope visits and speaks with leaders of other faith groups and they visit and speak with him, and the Church proclaims that it rejects nothing of what is true in any other religion. In communities all over the world, Catholics and Protestants and Orthodox who would barely acknowledge each other's presence in a former age are joining together to minister to the poor and build the kingdom of God. The continuing, difficult, sobering work toward unity is important to all of us, but it's one good reason to be glad we're Catholic today.

11 YOUTH

Two high-school-age boys worked for their parish after school and on summer vacations. They mowed lawns, waxed floors, and did other custodial work, all under the supervision of the parish sexton, a kind and gentle man named Ed.

Then Ed got very sick and couldn't work. With no long-term disability coverage and no salary, his young family would soon be in real trouble.

The two boys went to the pastor. You don't have to replace Ed, they said. We'll fill in for him. We'll make sure everything gets done just like he was here. No extra pay for the extra work—just keep Ed on the payroll.

The pastor agreed. The two boys kept their bargain, and Ed kept his salary.

Time and again in my life I've been surprised and strengthened by true stories of supposedly self-centered young people stepping up, handling responsibility, and working for causes greater than themselves. And in the past few years I've had the privilege of working with some amazingly talented young Catholics who take their faith very seriously and want to make a difference in the world.

They are a true gift to our Church, a gift recognized by Popes John Paul II and Benedict XVI, who have met with our youth in World Youth Days and other gatherings and have challenged them to approach faith, and their witness to the world, in ways that really matter.

Of course, not every young person responds. A lot of parents and grandparents are worrying these days because their children have stopped going to church. It is painful to watch a child turn away from something that has given the parent such life. All any of us can do is to love and pray for our children, continue to strive to live a Christ-centered life ourselves, and trust that God loves our children even more than we do and never gives up on them.

We plant the seed of faith. Someone else waters it, and

someone else reaps the harvest, and it all happens in God's time. God is in charge, not us, and that should always give us reason to be glad, and to live in joyful hope.

12 MARY AND THE SAINTS

"I'm not talking to Saint Francis," Peter told me.

"Why?" I asked. "What did he do?"

"I planted my spring garden and asked Francis to watch over it. Then the late freeze came and killed everything."

"Does Francis know you're mad at him?" I asked. "He sure does," replied Peter. "I turned his garden statue around so it faces the wall. He can stare at the bricks until I'm ready to forgive him."

Someone who didn't know Peter might think he's a bit daft. But if he is, it's in a charming, Catholic sort of way. Peter knows that the statue isn't magically alive. But he takes his gardening very seriously, and, like many Catholics, he has developed a very human relationship with his personal saints, with all the ups and downs that human relationships can have. He shares his joys and frustrations with them, and when he feels they haven't acted like good friends, he isn't afraid to call them out on it.

Statues aren't alive, of course, but saints are. They live

in the presence of our Lord and intercede for us. Their roles as inspirers, role models, helpers, and friends are rooted deeply in the Catholic heart. They are the great cloud of witnesses surrounding us and praying for us—and praying *with* us in Christ when we gather for Eucharist. We are all united in the Church, which spans heaven and earth.

And of our saints, there is none greater than Mary, the mother of Jesus, the Mother of God. Devotion to her sprang up very early in our history, and it remains strong today. Mary is our spiritual mother as well—the mother of the Church, the first disciple of her Son, and the model of discipleship for us all.

All kinds of Catholics connect to Mary, because she seems to speak to us in so many ways—mothers, fathers, widows, anyone who's had their life turned upside down, anyone who's lost a child, anyone who's been unfairly pushed around, anyone whose faith has been challenged. Mary knows firsthand what we're going through, and knows what it means to say "yes" to God. And while we sing of her as meek and mild, no one can go through all she went through without an inner strength that can come only from God.

Reacting to excesses in Catholic piety, the Protestant reformers turned away from Mary, but today more and more Protestant writers are rediscovering her and holding her up as a model to follow, a friend to speak to.

And we should never forget that sainthood is never restricted to those canonized or in heaven. There are living saints in the making all around us, single or married, laity, clergy and religious, women and men courageously living in Christ by loving and serving others. They, too, like everything we've mentioned in this booklet, are a great reason to be glad you're Catholic.

The 12 interrelated reasons we've looked at so briefly here—community, Vatican II, spirituality, sacraments, Eucharist, prayer, justice and Christian witness, Scripture and Tradition, creeds and catechetical renewal, ecumenism, youth, Mary and the saints—are only the beginning. I hope you'll pick up where I've left off and shape your own list. Remembering all the great reasons to be glad we're Catholic can strengthen our faith and challenge us to live it more fully. It can bring us joy and hope. And it can inspire us when we're feeling worn down by our own failures and those of others in the Church. In those times we can lift up our hearts and thank God that (as St. Paul put it) "where sin increased, grace overflowed all the more" (Romans 5:20).

Also by Dan Connors

Our Parish at Prayer
A Prayerbook for Eucharistic Adoration
These vibrant prayers are full of life, love, reverence, and awe. Anyone who spends time in Eucharistic Adoration—or who would like to experience it more deeply—will enjoy this inspiring treasury of prayers.
32 PAGES | 99 CENTS | ORDER 958092
978-1-58595-809-2

Home Blessings
Honoring God's Presence in Every Room
These simple and beautiful reflections about the spaces in our homes and what we do in them are a lovely reminder of how graced we are to have and share these spaces.
32 PAGES | $2.95 | ORDER 957392
978-1-58595-739-2

1-800-321-0411
WWW.23RDPUBLICATIONS.COM